DATE DUE

BILLBOARD
in the
CLOUDS

poems by

Suzanne S. Rancourt

CURBSTONE PRESS

Printed in the U.S. on acid-free paper by BookMobile

Cover design: Stone Graphics

This book was published with the support of the
Connecticut Commission on the Arts and donations from
many individuals. We are very grateful for this support.

The author wishes to thank the following magazines in which some
of these poems first appeared: *The Albany Review, Callaloo, Cimarron
Review, Family Issues, Gatherings, Suntracks, Tamaqua* and *Through
the Eye of the Deer.*

Library of Congress Cataloging-in-Publication Data

Rancourt, Suzanne S., 1959-
  Billboard in the clouds / by Suzanne S. Rancourt.
    p. cm.
  ISBN 1-931896-08-9 (pbk. : alk. paper)
  1. Indians of North America—Maine—Poetry. 2. Racially mixed
people—Poetry. 3. Abenaki Indians—Poetry. 4. Nature Poetry. 5.
Maine—Poetry. I. Title.
PS3618.A48B57 2004
811'.6—dc22   2003027087

published by
  CURBSTONE PRESS 321 Jackson Street Willimantic, CT 06226
      phone: 860-423-5110 e-mail: info@curbstone.org
              http://www.curbstone.org

There are so many to whom this book of poems is dedicated. There is my Mother whose warrior spirit is the mover of all obstacles that drives me to be myself as Creation intended. There is my Father whose steadfast connectedness to the Natural World continues to feed my respect and admiration for the mountains and the people of them. There are my two sons for whom I hope I am a driving force just as my Mother was and still is for me. There is my Sister who never stops believing in me. And there are my many Dance Brothers and Sisters, Warrior Brothers and Sisters, my Drum family. There are the many, many fine Elders and Teachers who give of themselves honestly, freely, respectfully. There are those friends who are family and have supported me throughout the years as we have supported each other. And the mountains that I go home to every night. This book is dedicated to all of you.

Table of Contents

I

II

III

Billboard in the Clouds

I

Soft

it was that subtle
the way we wrap our hands around warm clay mugs
the way we close our eyes before we drink fresh brewed coffee
the way we narrow a smile to keep the cold from hammering
our teeth
the way we curve our wrinkled fingers
around our own shoulders
thinking of someone else

Sometimes, We Get Lucky

We were watching a meteorite shower
and I said, "A person couldn't wish this much"
but that was before a star got lost in my hair
bruised its way into my head and made of it
a cheesehead soufflé to which
Julia Childs would add parsley.

Cooking with Julia
isn't much different than living with you,
my stale mate,
which isn't much different
than friggin' with a roll of cheap saran wrap
where the beginning or end is never found—
the way we argue.

Savor the intoxicating dryness.
We often drink red wine while it is still breathing
until there's no breath left in the room and we don't
have to wonder what its nature would be in outer space.

In outer space
the wine could be bled weeks in advance
drop by drop
strung out in space to lead
to an empty cork
suspended where last touched
like when you want sex and don't get it.

As weightless as the cork itself
we could float around with our mouths hung open
trying to dock with a microscopic dram—
not much different from our mornings when we try

to scoop refined sugar
into our coffee cups and stir.

You prefer just Cremora
but its atmospheric swirl
offers no indication of weather
or why we need artificial life support systems.
And like you, my genital nervousness does not explain
why some things need free oxygen and anaerobiums do not.
One lives freely and the other
bottled and sealed
expected to ferment for the mere pleasure of consumption.

Whose wine are you still drinking?
And how could our Lazy Susan lives ever mix in this space
where shooting stars are too many
where a person could bleed to death forever?

Embryonic Weave

men
have said i have nice skin
they want to touch
with poignant eyes
and hands
as if to question the existence of my flesh
to make sure it is real
the aesthetics of sensation

i know this
the way i know the obsession
of the fetal curl
the possessive tug of plush blanket
coddling
its satin trim
its silken security
near mouth
and thumb

Even When the Sky Was Clear

My father talked to the clouds.
He knew when the snow would come
how much and for how long,
what kind of rain
and the wind that would bring it.

I would watch him
through my mother's kaleidoscopic den windows,
immaculate and sparkling,
I'd rush from the table, crayons, or t.v.
Or from my rock sentinels holding my hand-hewn poplar bows and spears
or while perched amongst and atop my White Pine, I'd watch,
or with my feet buried in the peak of the sand pile.
I would watch my father
stand in the center of the dooryard appropriately round
in red and black checkered wools
or in a tee shirt mottled with holes from cutting-torch sparks.
Everything still and listening,
except for an occasional Crow's caw or Blue Jay,
or the tiniest sound of the first few snowflakes landing
or the muffled hiss of blanketing fog in its subtle turn to pre-rain mist.

Even in the summer
he'd look to the clouds, to the sky
at dawn, at dusk.

Now,
I stand in a circle.
There's a Tree in the center dressed in brilliant colors,
sometimes, I leave sweet things there and let the shadows touch me.
There's a drum and singers,
sometimes, I hear them.

Sometimes, I don't
because I am singing to the clouds
in the language
my father
taught me.

South Wind in the Big Horns

So
one day wind
just changed direction
now
it blows
as a puff of breath
a child's breath
and a flap of pudgy-fingered hands
impetus for the soundless motion
of a bird mobile
dangling over a crib in a corner of a room
any room—

As though it were
from many mouths whose tongues
have been replaced
by the multicolored strips of cloth scarves, shirts,
pouches, bags, and baubles
tied by generic hands
to a chainlink fence and barbed wire holding together
a wheel of stones   a nation of people
wafts of tobacco lick the steel netting
a cat cleaning a wound.

As though it were
just glancing the tops of empty beer bottles
stacked outside on the porch—any porch—
this same breath
fondles a cluster of forged tubes
dangling from the ceiling of the same porch
hollow bones
aluminum reeds
waiting

for the essence of an unseen miracle
to make it all tangible
like a voice
waiting for a throat.

Efun

The faces were sad, she said, they are the daddies.
She doesn't like to swing high and made a tall tower
of blocks calling it a boat
with a door and curtains
and drawing a rainbow
the child pretended that the houses talked.
In the driveway, using inventive spelling,
she wrote her story in chalk.

Who Strings the Bow?

he pulls two chairs to the table.
lunch time, the sky
is still grey. a steady garden rain hangs in the pines
before it is gravity-sucked into the earth.
everyone must be fed
and the plush nose of Blackie
the valore puppy
is placed lovingly inside
a Raggedy Ann + Andy lunch box
her thermos
a 3-D viewmaster, filled
with fluid glimpses of Seseme Street.

he is five, my son, and says "I love you, Mom,
but I can't tell you this" and raises
his flapping-Raven-wing-eyebrows
four times. he pats
the pseudo-ravioli with a clean spoon
swirls the red sauce and spiraling cheese
"Mom, is it possible
to be a bow and an arrow
at the same time?"

When the Air Is Dry

the insects buzz and saw
through heat waves.
Pepere knows it's time
to work the fields.
he stares at the sun.

these memories are distant
yet as shadows leak through pine needles,
the way milk drips between the leaves of a table,
they continue to seep
into my heart and home
of hand braided rugs
and rocking chairs,
through my mind
into my children's lives.

to be fluid as wind
that sprawls over silvery July grasses…I need…
but cannot smell the scent
of sweet, sweet, fresh cut hay, again, and the sun
burns the nape of my neck.
I have stacked bales of green hay
into little pyramids dotting open pastures,
they wait for the Farmall with its wagon
and splintered racks.
the muscles on my back tighten over ribs, a runner's ribs,
living sinew, breathe and glide
over skeletal ridges and valleys
baling twine cuts my hands, blood arroyos to my fingertips
and chaff settled in my pants. I remember

the hay
always weaved its way
into my hair,
making a wreath of it—the hat, the hair—
our skin brittle as dry leaves from wind-kissed sweat

what is it that stops moving when the sun sets?
what is it that spins inside my head and in my belly?

a dragonfly's
holographic vision coats
my past and future
with the iridescence of unexplained knowing.

why am I just standing in the middle of the field?
I've lost sight of the tractor's sound
I'm no longer where the voices are
the sun pounds my childish panic into its descent beyond
the silhouette of trees.
I hear singing

I raise my hand
to grasp a wisdom
children lose
when language
is beaten out of them.

The Incredible Shrinking Bike

Have you ever noticed how fucking incongruent humans are?
It got summed up one morning in the unJuly-like
                                  Appalachian rain at the five-way
intersection. There was a fellow on a bicycle—something about his hair—
don't know if it was punk or if he just didn't know enough to comb it.
Kinda stood up on end like penguins teetering
his hair spikes rocked with his pedaling and wind.
Don't know if he was Aryan or Dutch or neither but his hair
was that blond and his eyes that blue and I recalled Lusanne Switzerland:
cows tongue and french mustard sauce. My son's diaper
                              dropped around his sandaled feet
on Main Street, and no one cared. It was summer
                              and I didn't stay long enough.
A language of regrets sung across fields of alfalfa and poppies.
I go there often as a wind of grief like the corner of a mouth
                              threatening to smile.
With the headiness of a Choucas'* caw, an avalanche
                              rumbling to the coast
of cold water and standing stones. Displacement is an act.

A pick-up truck with a single-hinged tailgate lurched from a pot hole
and startled a swerve from the bicyclist, a snappy tick
                              of a tumbling glance cartwheeled
over an art deco epaulet. His eyebrows, dark brown, troweled together
plowing through an adolescent face. But the bike was too small
and he strained to peddle it, his legs, too long and gangly and his knees
rising up out of his lap banged the handle bars. The bike was so small
he looked like a body with feet, like those pop up bauble toys
you gavel down with a fist, Little Bunny Phoo Phoo, and wait
for their explosive googliness teetering stiffly at its full height.
Long two legs, a child not a child, strained

*choucas: ravens that live at extraordinarily high altitudes.

15

to work too late, maybe, and hurrying.
Clownish adolescent twenties at the five way intersection—
                                        stunts that don't fit.
But Acrobat Bear he was not in his black leather jacket,
                                        chrome chains, shirt tails flapping
two thirds untucked, offering the pencil holder of his ass-crack.
There he was
Easy Rider boots and spurs, pant legs two-thirds tucked in:
the little red bike kept getting centrifugally smaller
                                        as he hugged the curb
chased by dogging time and nipping cars.
His face mottled by cramping gut and panic
twisting his neck, flesh rolled up into his brow cornrowed with anguish
dry teeth earmarked his lips to a snarl—pitbull of a charlie horse—
dry heaves would be a blessing, but he knows
that instant, he knows, his bicycle is too small.
Penguins were made to fall,
and the Shriners are coming...There, take the picture now!
                                        Now! Now! Take it...

Thunderbeings

While gazing through a window for a split-atomic second,
my grandmother, was struck and killed by lightning.
Her left finger touching one of the four brass posters
as gently as one touches the cheeks of newborns
as though she had pressed a doorbell,
a button on an elevator —ascend please—
then the lightning arched and she crossed over
leaving a fingerprint
and a strong smell of uric acid.

Her name was Dorothy, an artist
taught by the nuns. She painted in oils
the light and dark of all things—
ships full sail on calm oceans—
I could not reach them, hanging on the wall,
so I'd pull a chair under these two paintings
one new moon dark, the other full moon light—
I would press my finger on each brush stroke, each sail
wondering where these ships were sailing
in my Memere's head.

Her name was Dorothy, a Parisienne farm woman, I was told,
who on bad days when the horse and carriage
couldn't make the hard scrabble to Mass
would open up the parlor and hold her own, chanting Hail Mary's.

The next year the lightning
came back, took the barn, took the horses.
The bed, where my cooling Memere had lain the year before
was removed from the house, stored in the shed
until forty years later when I polished for days
the spokes and posters. A brass lamp of sorts
illuminated images of a woman

I never knew. I rubbed
until the chalky, thunderhead blue dissolved
and the metal shone lightning yellow.
For years I slept in this bed,
and often heard her
still humming in the brass.

Crystal Hawk Song

The finger
must be conditioned
slightly moist
and applied delicately to the lip
of the crystal bowl
as to the edge of a razor.
When balance has been achieved
Hawk Song screams loudest.

From a distance
a white breast is perched
on more than one
precocious perspective.

Getting to the meat of the matter—

It's more than who folds the laundry:
it's fear
of everything I want to be
and the shadow on the field of knowing
that it takes more
than pretentious demanding
to angle flight
from youth to wisdom.

Little Birds

they jump rope with an umbilical cord
and chant with each skip
"Red Bird sings in the morning
Red Bird awakens me"

the ever- watching-shawl-draped-grammas
peer deep between the dialogue
of lowered eyes
and lustful glance.

and watch
little girls no more.
their seed pod bellies swell
like breasts of birds.

into nests
glitter-dreams glass birds do weave
and songs, Red Bird sings
in the morning
in the morning
let down
your voluptuous-raindrop-seed-pearl-notes
from water's heaven
moisten my heart   i pray
for rain, tip back my bird head   i scry*
the sun, words are not enough.

i forgot how to sing.

*scry, to scry, scrying—a gazing technique to foretell the future.

Whose Mouth Do I Speak With

I can remember my father bringing home spruce gum.
He worked in the woods and filled his pockets
with golden chunks of pitch.
For his children
he provided this special sacrament
and we'd gather at this feet, around his legs,
bumping his lunchbox, and his empty thermos rattled inside.
Our skin would stick to Daddy's gluey clothing
and we'd smell like Mumma's Pine Sol.
We had no money for store bought gum
but that's all right.
The spruce gum
was so close to chewing amber
as though in our mouths we held the eyes of Coyote
and how many other children had fathers
that placed on their innocent, anxious tongue
the blood of tree?

II

Haunting Fullblood

I.

Oh, Indian woman that sold butter,
Rispah,
my unsettled blood
speak to me through the generations
of crossed out names and altered paperwork.

Rispah, Grandmother to grandmothers
whose grave cannot be found
perhaps you never died
but simply traveled
to another place and time—
perhaps you returned to your people, your ways,
that no one spoke of.
In a pasteboard box, at someone's wake, buried among
your framed in-laws and children's children
my hand found you—you found me.

Were you anything more than a photograph?
Oh, yes, Rispah, Grandmother, my subtle bridge
over flooding time—shhh—
I am breathing proof.

II.

there is something hard in my cheek bones.
sharp like Eagle beaks.

when i release my breath
to the grey and motionless sky
something behind my facial planes

melts
into meandering notes of a soprano sax,
washes
into droplets,
trickles down the keyboard, flat ivory,
gentle rain on river,
where my grandmothers bathed
and the rocks
are that smooth.

Even on Lark Street

The shadow
the smoke stack dragged as a nylon stocking
or a rumpled varicose vein.
Or, was it the smoke's wind-sock-shadow that clipped
the guardrails like playing cards clothes pinned to a bicycle
fork drumming the spokes incessantly as partridge.
And the whole thing, tractor trailer and all, in spite
of its high buff chrome stacks and spin-balanced Homeric hubs
are stifled, an odorless shadow, like a harpist's fingertips strumming
the landscape, or a hangnail tearing the sunset.
Or, perhaps, it's more like a shin shaved too quickly
with too much wrist that *gee* and *aws* this big rig
that snagged itself along 787 and sucked me
through downtown where I drove by her
every morning on Lark Street.

But I always get a little dissociative when I'm in the city.
At first glance I saw her exhale at 10 below
waiting for a bus.

On the west end of town
the wingnut who sold us our house took two in the chest,
lead ripped through his clothing and heart,
snagged his spine, riffling his ribs and he crumpled
to the ground, a pile of remnants: the Owl was done with him.
What did he expect?
And the shadow of the cop he'd pinned with his back
bumper to the front of the cruiser reeled, his pistol spun
like thumb twizzlers from Sugar Pops in the '60s.
Or, Roy Roger's guns, but they were shiny, this pistol
was blue. Like forever young Gene Autry's voice, even when
he was happy, he just sang and it was the women

who swooned and crumpled to the ground
not like this crazy guy dressed in a powder blue
polyester suit, wide lapels and black platforms and the cop
whose gun spun like a bottle and time and the dizziness
you feel in the head when you realize you've sat
through the green light:

Sometimes,
I'd make extra trips down Lark Street
to see if she was still waiting for the bus.
Her Africanness wrapped regally in her twisted turban of gold
and red paisley leaked out from under her
black, leather coat in rippling python waves, like waves
lapping a trade ship's hull, spilled
on a winter's mukluks, liked a dropped beer, a hot coffee,
displaced on a snow, a frozen melted hole like half-sucked sugar,
gray and squeaking with each
evolutionary cold-after-cold step but never stepping
on the bus. She just smoked and exhaled—
the barrel of a cooling gun, a fluted crepe, a pie from the oven,
a smoke stack, a pressure cooker, a howitzer,
a long stemmed pipe, a steaming kettle, my son's teddy bears
when the crazy guy placed the lamps too close to them.
I guess he must have had dreams of owning the house himself
or, maybe he thought the teddy bears were cold.

How crazy is it to miss your childhood?
How crazy is it to break into peoples' houses?

Behind the barn,
by the creek, it's always quiet even when
the kingfisher's F-10 belly flies below the ground line
inches above the water's surface tracking fish.
What I didn't know then, ten years ago when we bought the house:
he really was crazy.

Les Montagne

higher than most airplanes fly
i stood
in the french alps
my breath soared
through space so thin
even my flesh
would have enjoyed peeling
in a fruity sort of way
like the taste of that blue alpine flower
the mountain folks made liquor from
"everything will get you drunk"
they spoke their own language
"so you might as well drink this too"
we all smiled and watched
my toddling son splash in the spring.

we were all on the edge of something
that our different tongues spoke little of,
but our eyes
always wandered to the glaciers,
rested on the Choucas
that circled between sharp peaks and july corn snow.
we looked to the villages minusculed in creviced depths
below and distant
we drank and drank
kept searching and touching
each others eyes
knowing
that as we drank the mountains
we drank each other.

Not the Same Dream

fan
hawk's wing spiraled
Sky to Earth
hands,   it landed
in my hands,   pulsed,
it landed,   closed, my eyes closed
mouth opened   millenniums
millenniums   persecution
wailed unclutched and wailed   palm
to palm hands, my
hands, rose from them, a   wing
and bent into a Great,
Raven feather,   a sickle,
a bridge,   a bent bow,   a
many colored bow,   you,   you
found me,   my hands

This Breath We Are

Gramma,
the other day, i draped myself
in a wool shawl and cried
the stories in your eyes
i remembered.

"Why?"
he said
there on the water bed
our universal pool of queen-size love
that we agree to share
as we share each other's breath.

"What is its meaning, its symbolism, this Pipe?" he said
and pressed his cheek upon the crown of my head.

It is winter.
The evening spreads quickly
its darkness into our heartbeat of questions
just days ago
i placed my hands on the small of his back
for hours,
his pain, he said, left
with the first touch
and my hands
he said
sank into a relationship
where he knew we were separate but one
as he slipped into a bowl of unconsciousness
and woke
with a vision.

Eleanor

I found your diet spoon wrapped in cobwebbed dolies
pressed like yellow Tansy and repellent Pennyroyal
between swollen pages thick as tongues – your diary –
pressed between moments and paragraphs
pressed as a pill to the roof of your mouth
choked away in a peddler's truck – your trunk –
dusted with foreign baggage claims.
Tie dyed t-shirts concealed your German Crystal
 coddled your cobalt, stained-glass wind chimes
and smothered your butterfly magnets.
It all rotted slowly in the bone dry dirt, under
the kitchen floor, a root cellar,
you left everything for someone else
to dispose of. "It wasn"t easy" you wrote,
"to make the decision" although
you never said why.
Eleanor,
I took your rocking chair.
The landlord said I stole it.
My babies were crying. I needed to rock them.
Eleanor,
I don't know why you killed yours.

The Sorrows of the World Are Not Yours to Keep

in this you are the fist
not the white knuckles clenched as teeth to robes
and sashes and buttoned vestments.
i don't need to see your face
to know that you are black and white and greyscale and square
as the angle of your fingers clamped, meticulous, tight and
direct as the jaw you strike.
you are the fist of frustration
the fist of anger
the fist of hatred
your are the fist clutching seeds
clutching hope
clutching dreams
clutching sorrow

Sowing

What is tucked in the black void
of my skirt ruffles
is the Cave to a woman's soul.

Listen
to its parastaltic roll singing
up from the heart
or down from the Womb—
the same throat
it is.

Warrior Women

Dance women dance
    someone reads
our feet burn in dirt
    a poem about Mary and Martha
we never leave the Earth
    we live in the woods
our hearts are leaping fire
    we lay with mountains
our breath singing wind
    scream with Bear
our pulse is drumming life
    and give our menses to Maka
our laughter rings with wisdom
    bleed
Dance women dance
    from our womb-void
Hey Ya
    dark creation
Hey Ya
    streaked with white sunrise
Hey Ya
    bursting birth
Hey Ya

Behind the Beaded Curtains

And this room is just the way I want it to be used
now that I've hung the white cloth and removed the meticulously
tight braids of sweet grass:
My cumulus mind
and scratchy throat offer blessings
the futon that sits where the Steinway sat for years here
even longer there, like a Hitchcock twist, a mystery mantle —
now you see it now you don't
emergent hole, Sipapu, that migrated
an entire household toward peace.
Maybe it was the revolutionary solder decals
on the Steinway that didn't fit
or the ugliest veneering-entertainment-center-gone-bookcase in the world
with its funeral-parlor-pallor in the family room
that simply did not fit where the palm tree does
sprawling its fronds above the pink flamingos, aluminum legs,
stalking vermiculite funk and the power to be in it.

The Blessing

Resisting resurrection on the horizon the sun
hung as a blazen Blood Orange.

Blood Oranges
tasted sweetest by the Fountain de Trevi.

My lips thinned with sunset, drew back from my teeth
as night's fingers brushed back cloud's veil
from a crescent moon—

And my chin and fingers, sticky with fragrance,
we licked them for taste.
I did not want to wash, even though
it was Easter in Rome.
I did not want to resist the seduction
of the soil in the flesh
as lush and wet as the meat of the Oranges
we peeled with our teeth.

Poolside Manna

It was a simple aquacise that anyone could do
but you seem a little too jovial and pale.
Your knubby knuckles gesticulated too nimbly
you and your senior lady friends chatted too sociably
then they screamed—

My heart beat for both of us.
I knew what I had to do
and blasted the guard whistle more sharply
than any hearing aid feedback.
Everyone tried to hoist themselves from the water
their skin sagging with their swimsuits.
They cried for you and all others their age.
I could see what they were thinking in their kind, doughy faces
that another one of them had left,
so they huddled more closely, shivering on the pool deck
as children during a long swim lesson,
their mouths making noises
like the water in the pool's gutters.
I placed you on my hips and back
and felt your weight as I stepped from the water—
putty flesh, loose breasts. An arm hung over my shoulder
and its hand swung, a pendulum
striking my younger thighs
and I heard the water trying to pull us back,
trying to keep us
but your hand kept ticking—
I had four minutes to make you live,
even though you may not have wanted me to.
It's my job.

Your bathing cap and its quirkish latex flowers fell off
exposing your spiked and bluish hair,
your lips were that color.
My mouth covered them—yours were already cold.
again, again, again—live and live and live—
Your breastbone resisted
but I didn't stop until something in your face twitched—
a grandchild's birthday, an appointment, something in the oven—
your mouth sputtered
as though you were spitting out words,
sour, puckering words.
I drew breath for both of us
and told you so.

Dance

my legs are explosions
expressions
of lustful wind
i converse through cracks in the walls
slipping in my true intention like a snow drift
on the inside
side of a door i pound
your chest
has become my wailing wall
i crave your tongue dusted
with words and implications
i have something you need

A Light Wind Beyond Temple

—for Denise

Our shadows of existence were closer
than either of us realized for whatever reason.
The boundaries—vague, nebulous—maintained,
or stirred by my father's snow plow.
The only one willing to keep your roads open.
How this thought intrigues me thirty-five years later
perusing your poetry collections, essays and organic forays.
Would you have made it to the airports? New York City?
Europe, California? Would you have made it to your lectures and
demonstrations?
Did you even know my father's name?

My father was always concerned about the people
living at the end of dirt roads. How would anyone get to you
in case of an emergency?

He buried a horse after it strangled itself
from panic and barbed wire
when know one else would.

He buried a Jewish woman before sunset.
He didn't break ground until told to
and wouldn't leave the door yard
to make sure he was home when her husband called.
He didn't understand it, he said, it just had to be done that way.

Your husband, Mitch, knew my father's name.
My father knew yours too but simply referred to you
and your friends as the "crazy Russians."

This, of course, was prior to the confirmation
that his youngest daughter was more like you than not.
But so was my father.
That's why he made sure
your roads to the world were always open

Take From My Hair—Memories of Change

today
a rake drags across my forehead—
it is August.

we used to migrate
down the coast and up through the central mountains—-
a many-tined people,
we'd "j" our way to the foot of Katahdin—
a wind-ribbon of people,
we'd scoop our sustenance into ash baskets
that tourists preferred to buy unstained
and without blue berries—
the times changed
our men bent as willows,
our women strapped with foresight

why now
do i look for blueberries?
i strain to hear my language
among the leathery leaves
among the trees and trails that
my grandmothers and grandfathers walked
i keep thinking that i see them
walking toward me, i keep thinking that
i feel them touching me when my back is burdened sore
or when my rake swings sluggish
there in the fields of rhythmic silence
i have time to think
and remember what i think
i recall

when i'd rather look
for a shadow to become one
with a stone wall
and low shrubs
on steep hills among
ledge outcrops
moss sundried
but at sunrise there is dew, by noon
everyone has gathered pounds
of purple berries that stay remarkably cool as
the cases of jostled soda
trucked over rutted roads in the back of rusted out pickups
creaking through fields and fields of time
and hunched, brown backs
one arm braced on a knee
the other combs for berries
and we'd sway—elephant heartbeat—
as slow as the sound of dew-soaked pantlegs
walking toward us

no one liked to be the first in the fields
no one wanted
to tell the bears

a bigger beast
now walks the land

Billboard in the Clouds

when the trees take so much pity on us
that their tears fall like raindrops
look up
tilt your bird-head back
mouth open and receive
these droplets of blessings
for they come from the purest
of origins
these jewels
are crystalline clean
the water sweet and alive
pray hard
so there will be no day
when their pity
is the only water we know.

III

Smything

Beetles, worms, centipedes—
tunneling fingers seeking life.
Snakes and moles pressing up out of—reaching magic—
flight of frost and cold, breath and fog and dragon's
unseen wind of birth whirling, whipping into sacredness
still
funneling through crevices around windows, doors and thoughts.

A young man twenty years ago while watching me write songs asked,
"Where do all the songs come from?"

Crackling smell of wood and white hot rocks
flare, flaming nostrils
lava, volcanic blood vibrates into part of, all of
flooding hips, gateways of glory, beauty, power and downfall.

This horse we ride its girth of life.

Who are we now annealed by sweet water for blessings?
Fish for blessings
stones for blessings
smooth as breasts for blessings
spring forth as new words for blessings
bubbling into the flesh of plants
the flesh of animals
for blessings
go to the river, kneel, cradle in your hands
your face- my face-
rinse away the salts of labor
and the deathing of life, of change and sorrows.

Sweet water, sweet water,
incarnate as satin for the soul
seduce us whole
sweet water, sweet water.

Where the Apples Fall

Somehow
I feel safer
knowing that I've buried the Grouse
among the roots
of the apple tree
where children play kickball
and swing from branch to branch
their arms looped like coat hangers
or question marks.

Around the base of the tree
a troddened circle is uncovered.
All the children know
is that it feels good to be there.

Ishnanti

(She Lives Alone)

It was a new ritual
this eating mangos as the sun rose.
The first predawn incision
made with a slicing silence
cradling the form in the palm of her hand.
The blood of it—sweet and sticky—
attracting bats, ants, and children.

Holding its ovalness
she wonders about breasts full of milk
and the little girl that didn't live.
One steady cut
bisecting to the pit from end to end
or side to side—a clean, crescent cut.

And so every month there is a ritual
and the bleeding women live alone,
the grief sucked from their bodies
in the stillness of letting it happen.

Bring to the mouth, flesh,
thick with pine taste, suckle with lips and truth—
dive deeper—the nose, the teeth—
the tongue penetrates the yellow-orange meat—
Breath biting breath.

To The Limits, Charles…Driving Ms. Mixblood

Today, I go fishing
job hunting tomorrow
another dozen applications, polite smiles and
over-perfumed hands shaking mine.
My resume is neat, clean, precise and loaded
with cryptic experiences to read as cave walls—
The interviewer's manicured finger interrogates the paper's edge.
Has my life been smooth enough?
She removes her glasses, queries, painted lips pursed, hen's asshole,
truth is she has no room for cavernous desire
to be concerned with the guano on her shoes:
the perches she has reached.

I climbed trees as a child, sat still for hours, glued
to my sanctuary vowing never to descend
and walk among the ordinary,
to remain at my post of denial.
I'd kick back with stained feet any encroachment of emotion:
A filthy-fat-girl, long-haired-wild-thing.

I had jack knives before all the boys.
My first knife, my mother gave me.
I made bows and spears,
played in the woods,
I had friends there.

Every evening my mother threatened with exasperated fear
that the shadows crept too near she threatened
to leave me there all night but she knew the owl flew close
and remembered
the two ominous birds stuffed and poised, looming
in the front room in her father's house

their crescent beaks gleamed as did their piercing talons:
The Red Tailed Hawk, the Great Horned Owl.

My father lured speechlessly with candies
he'd place them on a rock or a dish near the base of the tree
like setting out salt licks for deer
or plums for bear.

Today,
I lock myself in my car and create reasons to drive long distances
I kick back the city sludge drive into darkness
not knowing where I put my mourning dress.
I shroud myself with the mist of thunderheads and mountains
where there isn't any white smoke wound umbilically around my neck.
Another potato-rake of a lover gouges my human soul.
Everything is a lie
except the foggish gauze-wrapped river
and the broken guardrails.

Heron-man Passed Over

I want your tongue to run along my throat,
tantric knife,
passion pours forth
mix among the breath
of our past lives that I cannot release.
Paint your lips with my fear
speak them dry—
ghost—ghost

The Wisp

Driving down Broadway, Saratoga watching wind from my soundless car
snap locust branches—

a hallucinogenic motion melts into a canvas of rain,
dripping leaves crack as the whipping crest of salted waves.

The heat of a whip is cold. I recalled watching a movie as a child,
"The Summer of 42", Dorothy, sitting on stones at the shore,

like my Meme. Meme at Old Orchard. Meme
in the surrey. Meme in fur hat and muff. Meme

in black and white.
Meme in stories swirling through pine tops, pear trees and sweet grass,

a cool draft around the neck. Meme, Dorothy, struck by lightning
in the summer of '42.

Dorothy, sitting on stones at the shore writing letters
swells of hope, each word, the mouth rounds a murmur,

a prayer, a breath off the ocean in the hand
that brushed hair from the forehead, cradles the jaw,

fingers light on the neck. This woman who had the explorer's daring
to caress the rippling depths of innocence

awakens buried dreams: the dead will dance us.
Oh, glory be to a smile untainted and pure as a sliver of almond

grace to the dovish curve of lips, sweet trill to the tip of tongue and

Mimosa

and plums and memories…

I know this woman with the empty arms, the empty bed and a
telegraph. In the wake
of naïveté and grief we apply the salve of nothingness with the knowing

a soul acknowledges in tremoring rush after rush,
hollows silence and leaves us absent.

I Am Counting

from the center
of my grandmother's old spinning wheel's
wheel
hangs a corn kernel rosary
my hands
cracked and filled with motor oil,
seduce each seed for nourishment,
as though my hands were clam-digging
for lost pennies for postage stamps
in the bottom of my pocketbook.

each kernel
a condolence,
a time piece,
my thumbs tick off segments
the way I pull the beaded chain
on a ceiling light
like the one in the laundry room
that flickers
when the washer spins.

Sipping

—for my mother

It was not always bone china, the cup
the saucer, that your long feathered-fingered hands wrapped.
The cup, the saucer, holding
the moisture of an eggshell candling its papier-porcelainess to count
your shadowed maybes on the other side, like in the old days
when kerosene rags haloed your brow of buggy locks.
It only smelled as bad as it was.

No one really believed

the stories of burlap clothing fashioned from sugar—
flour- or potato sacks or that the lamb
really hung itself and its mother blatted for it
for days, her tits festered with grief that you
still added to your tea and stirred with a sterling spoon
bought with bottle money at a high end junk shop because you
could finally do that but no one really believed
the pastoral truth of poverty and trudging for miles
to a colder school than the walk through snow drifts
or the belly-down-face-first sled ride past Springer's
not the toboggan ride that broke your leg. You knew
no one had a spirit like yours. But no one
really believed it anymore than the sound of silent
precision of breath and the polyrhythms of chomping bits
and restless hooves while hitching up the team of horses
to the sleigh, buffalo lap blankets and all those brass bells—
gold gilt, brass bells, gold
rimmed your post-menopausal Currier and Ives
tea cups chattering on trays accompanied by different spoons
but still silver and embossed. "Com'boss!

Com'boss!" And who's boss on the farm
whose soil milked sweat and youth from the backs of boys,
their spines a stack of wafers: no more Canadian jigs.
All compressed into a bale of square-cornered hay
and stacks of photo albums and things you wanted to be
when you had enough desire to dream and hope.

Who would have guessed?

No more switchel* no more swinging scythe
no more Jimmie Stewart hay rides, no more no
more all in one square-cornered hay a kachunking machine
pursed forth a cube of nutrition, ready the black tea,
render the recollections of bitterness that you could not
set down:

Squirrels no longer fascinate me nor do people sitting
in parks or at city bus stops. Joggers
have become commonplace as knee pads
on roller bladers, or head phones, cell phones and
micro fiber. But nobody believes me either.

Who'd believe you'd die?

Only tea
tastes good piping hot from copper kettles,
mine is black, no English twist of milk,
just dark amber that only stark post-menopausal bone
china can appreciate with a tinkling curiosity
of what if's and sugar cubes the size of croutons
molasses tan and irregular like brown eggs
brought in from under the hen's ass in a child's hands
cradling the process before bigger hands crack it all
and somewhere between the delicate bird bites
of fresh bread and raspberry preserves the squeal
of a stuck pig became a seed betwixt your teeth and lard

on the palette your tongue dabbed unconsciously
and repeatedly painting on your retina the goofiness of horror:
a barking shadow-dog on a canvas tent wall,
the neighbor girl and her baby as they died
in a head-on collision. Who'd have guessed it was you
driving behind them and witnessed
the explosive ball of white light a microsecond prior to impact.
Sitting alone with a cup of tea was almost too much.

Whatever Greek poet said a heifer could be milked
was just damn wrong and no matter how you mixed it
the lamb still hung itself and you ate it.

*Switchel is an old farmers drink used when working in the fields to prevent
heat stroke and dehydration.*

Even in Keflavik*

Windows
peppered with construction dust, volcanic ash and fragmented pasts
shadowed spring rain and a rainbow appeared, cat-backed
across the Atlantic into Glasgow for fifteen minutes
made it easier for me to recount the dreams, review the details—
hair, clothing, body smells and tattoos.

 The process of breathing—
Contract, release, contract, release—
a torso releases into the thighs to escape the whipping past,
close to the Earth the sweat is thrown
to cast away the grief, the hardships—
to moisten the wisdom of sitting for days without food or water-
to wet the memory of sacrifice and to mark time
in our existence of hiking up the mountain over blow downs
                                        and over growth.
And continue, for whatever reason, to dance and murmur—
strength and beauty, strength and courage—and for whatever reason
I propelled forward through the loss of husbands and hope, false friends,
false promises, false impressions, false religions, false cultures,
                                        Campbell's soup,
tuna sandwiches and Sunday night Disney.

And even in fucking Keflavik
there were bomb threats, temporary walls, temporary stairs,
temporary schedules. And so, I sat there too
contemplating the preparation, the dreams
and the lying on my belly with no shade but The One sprig of sage
that I refused to set down while thinking I was dying,
wishing I was

*Keflavik, Iceland International Airport

and eating dirt like denial I told myself it was water and decided
that no buzzards gonna pick my ass and stood up
holding The One sprig of sage for whatever reason
and why not?
I walked into the shop that four years earlier
I knew I would four years later and asked questions about ink.

The artist showed me pictures—celtic knots, dolphins, butterflies,
                                        spiders, and skulls.
What did I have in mind? he asked, Did I see anything I liked?
Where did I want it?

What do you say to people? Its not about what I liked—
a Gumby on my belly or a pickle on my inner thigh.

So, six weeks later after planning and clarifying
not grizzly prints but black bear
not pit vipers but black rat snakes that spiral trees
with their pulsing undulations from earth to sky
like sap in the spring
and sweat after sweat, deliberation and consideration, finally
my day came in November with sleet, hail, thunder
and lightning hit with the first cut.
To the friend who came with me I said, "Do it now"
and she who had birthed six sons and I who had birthed two
began to breathe as slow as stones.
"It is my day" I said to the artist
who could not understand why his other clients never showed.
Eight hours—a day and a half less then the time it took to birth my sons
my body possessed by contractions, threw life forward, hurled stones
to the Earth, children to the world.

How does anyone prepare for anything?

The chisel crept up my spine as flames of goosebumps,
up and out of the Earth of my hips seeking

the canopy of wings to the grace of stars
and hands with no one to touch.

When did not touching or being touched become the norm?

How can compassion exist in a rattling chisel nailing ink to my spine,
lift off my shoulders with the touch,
that delicate sacred touch of an artist to the paper, my back,
a surgeon and scalpel
and the person I've never met lays their passion on my back,
hands of wind wipe away the colored sand, the healing done
                                        but never done.
The ink never lifted, the passion never dry and I called the guy
                                        the next day
and asked, " but when will the ink stop washing off?"
"Only a joke" I said, and then he laughed. Even in Keflavik the
                        shadows throw an Apgar arch into their back,
the vertebra, an abacus, didactic scores of moments
since last touched by a lover who spreads across my back
as a creation I never knew I missed until the indigo was
                                        tapped meticulously
into my flesh, rose to the top like foam in a bottle, incessant human needs—
an unobtrusive SOS,
as unobtrusive as slipping between the narrow bands of yellow-red sunrise,
as unobtrusive as the sharp Atlantic flatness,
or fingers circling a nipple, or hands following the bridge of an ileac crest
into the ancestral groin of fjords and lochs and even here
                                        in fucking Keflavik
volcanoes heave ice skyward.

Blossom For A Day

for all those who know Lupus (SLE)

Every time I close my eyes
I see poppies
orange and vocal with vibrancy
I see poppies
with a centered seed pod
I peer into them, my vision falling into—
no—I'm being sucked into
the volcano's vacuum
my mind dances on its rim
my feet sticky with pollen and regrets
leave tracks
upon the delicate petals of the past
I've lost my shoes
all I want to do is sleep
just let me sleep

Honor Song

there
in the box wrapped in red wool blanket   you there
on top of the flat cedar   you
in the white ash box   you
i sang you home   even though
it was night   i sang   songs   of the Sun
aunt tispit   and me   we drove
you   my mother   home my mother
i sang

out on the Hill   an Eagle lifted off at dawn
this i thought of that day you slipped   you
through the crack of day   your Soul
lifted off with the power
of a single drop   of water   on the tip
of a Choke   Cherry   leaf

Born and raised in west central Maine, Suzanne Rancourt is Abenaki, Bear Clan, and a veteran of the United States Marine Corps and the United States Army. Now a residence counselor for TBI, an organization in New York State aiding developmentally delayed and challenged individuals, she is a mentor for Wordcraft Writer's Circle, a singer-songwriter who has performed nationally, and an independent education consultant. Her work has appeared in literary journals such as *Callaloo* and *The Cimmaron Review* and has been widely anthologized. An earlier version of *Billboard in the Clouds* won the Native Writers' Circle of the Americas First Book Award in 2001.

A great advocate of the curative power of the arts, Ms. Rancourt holds a Master of Fine Arts degree in Poetry from Vermont College, and a Master of Science degree in Educational Psychology from SUNY-Albany, NY. She is also an herbal educator, percussionist, personal fitness trainer, and a performer/teacher of Middle Eastern and Afro-Caribbean dance. Presently living in Hadley, New York, she gives numerous readings and workshops in the Northeast.

CURBSTONE PRESS, INC.

is a nonprofit publishing house dedicated to literature that reflects a
commitment to social change, with an emphasis on contemporary writing
from Latino, Latin American and Vietnamese cultures. Curbstone presents
writers who give voice to the unheard in a language that goes beyond
denunciation to celebrate, honor and teach. Curbstone builds bridges
between its writers and the public – from inner-city to rural areas, colleges to
community centers, children to adults. Curbstone seeks out the highest
aesthetic expression of the dedication to human rights and intercultural
understanding: poetry, testimonies, novels, stories,
and children's books.

This mission requires more than just producing books. It requires ensuring
that as many people as possible learn about these books and read them. To
achieve this, a large portion of Curbstone's schedule is dedicated to
arranging tours and programs for its authors, working with public school
and university teachers to enrich curricula, reaching out to underserved
audiences by donating books and conducting readings and community
programs, and promoting discussion in the media. It is only through these
combined efforts that literature can truly make a difference.

Curbstone Press, like all nonprofit presses, depends on the support of
individuals, foundations, and government agencies to bring you, the reader,
works of literary merit and social significance which might not find a place
in profit-driven publishing channels, and to bring the authors and their
books into communities across the country. Our sincere thanks to the many
individuals, foundations, and government agencies who have supported this
endeavor: Connecticut Commission on the Arts, Connecticut Humanities
Council, Eastern CT Community Foundation, Fisher Foundation, Greater
Hartford Arts Council, Hartford Courant Foundation, J. M. Kaplan Fund,
Lamb Family Foundation, Lannan Foundation, John D. and Catherine T.
MacArthur Foundation, National Endowment for the Arts, Open
Society Institute, Puffin Foundation, United Way, and the
Woodrow Wilson National Fellowship Foundation.

Please help to support Curbstone's efforts to present the diverse voices and
views that make our culture richer. Tax-deductible donations can be made
by check or credit card to:
Curbstone Press, 321 Jackson Street, Willimantic, CT 06226
phone: (860) 423-5110 fax: (860) 423-9242
www.curbstone.org

IF YOU WOULD LIKE TO BE A MAJOR SPONSOR OF A
CURBSTONE BOOK, PLEASE CONTACT US.